The Ultimate Nightmare

SCRIPTOR HOUSE
THE EPITOME OF GREATNESS

JIM BRYANS

Scriptor House LLC

2810 N Church St Wilmington, Delaware, 19802

www.scriptorhouse.com

Phone: +1302-205-2043

Published by Scriptor House LLC

Paperback ISBN: 979-8-88692-264-6

eBook ISBN: 979-8-88692-265-3

Because of the dynamic nature of the Internet, any web addresses or links contained in this book may have changed since publication and may no longer be valid. The opinions expressed in this manuscript are solely the opinions of the author and do not represent the opinions or thoughts of the publisher and the publisher hereby disclaims any responsibility for them. The author has represented and warranted full ownership and/or legal right to publish all the materials in this book.

The Ultimate Nightmare

JIM BRYANS

Having considered the fact that a few years ago, I put this story on the internet. I decided to have another look and see just what I may have missed. Yes, I do think there were several vital points that after searching, came to light.

So herewith, is an update. They say that time is a great healer, and with all the years that have gone by, has the pain gone? Yes, of course, it has, but there is still an underlying, seething hatred for how the whole thing was dealt with by the perpetrators, and my defence in particular. They were quick to tell me it was a 'good result,' but, in the light of what I have found; I think it most certainly was not!

My story is about Penile Cancer, the pain and misery of being diagnosed with this horrible disease, but more importantly, it's about how after years of worry and distress, I was able to put it all behind me, to be absolutely, and completely cured, and find peace of mind; that was a dream come true. Following a brief period of joyous relief, to have my dream shattered and wake up to the horror of suffering what they termed as 'a Medical accident' which in effect, obliterated all the good work done by a team of surgeons, and then to have the Hospital deny it for seven years. Even though this story was featured on TV in programs called 'Medical Horrors,' 'Hospital Stories from Hell,' and was rated the very top in another program called: '99 Most Bizarre surgical screw ups.' They didn't even scratch the surface. The pain and distress of cancer, followed by the horror of the Medical Accident paled in the wake of the denial and the court case, which for me was: 'The Ultimate Nightmare,' and left a beast within me that will never go away.

Jim Bryans

You never dream that a bizarre turn of events could change your entire life in a way that seems irrevocable. Even though Jim suffered 'The Ultimate Nightmare,' and despite the agony he faced daily for seven long years, he had to put on a brave face and deal with the task of bringing up his six birth children and four adopted children, three of whom had very special needs with no speech. He felt that the horror he was suffering should not overshadow the love of his family or jeopardise their security. When he was certain he was dying, he had no alternative other than to have a heart-to-heart with them. They were shocked and distressed; they wept as they kissed him goodbye. Jim's story is unique; this has never happened to anyone else and let us hope that it never will again!

CONTENTS

Prologue

I was the youngest child of four, born in Belfast three years before the start of World War two. I lived with my Mum, two brothers and a sister. My father, who, while World War 1 was in progress, joined up as a boy soldier, re-enlisted at the outbreak of World War 2 and didn't return until the end of the war.

We lived in a quite nice area and were reasonably well off; considering the times. When Belfast was bombed during Easter of 1941, our house suffered slight damage, but luckily, we escaped and were evacuated to a farm some thirty-five miles north of Belfast; by that time, I was four. The others were all at school, so the farmer took me under his wing, and treated me like his son. He took me everywhere with him and as a result, I began to regard him as my Daddy; how I loved him!

Upon our return to Belfast, we ended up in a really deprived area, and because of family problems, my father took to the bottle, and we went penniless. Pining for the farmer, I yearned to go back to the farm, and later on, I became something of a problem child.

My poem that follows is a quite accurate description of how things turned out. I was put in the care of an extremely tough children's home, where the strong ruled the weak. Over the years, we received training on a daily basis to a high degree and, I adapted so well that by the age of sixteen, I was among the toughest boys in the school.

Three years or so after my release, at about the age of eighteen, during a scuffle, while attempting to squeeze my testicles, a boy squeezed my penis. Despite a lot of bruising, I thought that I had emerged unscathed, but this was to come back and haunt me in later life.

During a check-up, a doctor told me I should go in for a small operation (that I thought was unnecessary) to correct a problem when going to the toilet, and I suffered what they termed as 'a Medical accident,' or as it was referred to during the court case that followed as: 'an unnecessary procedure.'

The intervening years were extremely harrowing and debilitating; I received no aftercare from the hospital, other than periodical check-ups during which I was not even examined, but invariably asked: 'Still using the catheter?' Then I was sent on my way. It seemed to me that I was a problem no one wanted to see.

Everyone, including the national press, said that I won my case, but I think they just tossed a few quid in my direction so that I would go home and shut up, However, as you can see, here I am again. This article is supported by scrupulously recording details on my computer, and as far as I can recollect, my interpretation of the events that took place is completely accurate. I am eighty-six years old, married for over sixty-years. I have some wonderful memories but then again, on the other hand, some not quite so wonderful as this article explains in graphic detail. This was a very traumatic period in my life, thankfully it is now over, although the after taste is something that will never go away. It is fair to warn you that it does contain graphic photos and owing to its very nature, is of an adult theme as it concerns penile cancer. Any one of you out there who are at present going through this, has to be suffering what prior to my so-called medical accident, I would have considered, 'The Ultimate Nightmare.' I think that contained herein is what I would have thought of as valuable information that I wished I'd had all those years ago, perhaps my life could have been very different.

Chapter 1

This poem epitomises my early years putting you in the picture:

Kids

Us kids, we were so rough and tough in Belfast's city streets.

Times were hard and food was scarce, we hadn't any treats.

Two up, two down, that's where we lived, bare boards throughout the house.

Our only entertainment was if our cat would catch a mouse.

Our bed, that was another thing, no blankets there to fold,

No sheets, just heavy overcoats to keep us from the cold.

We had no larder, just a cupboard, and that was always bare.

The only thing we had was salt, or sometimes lard was there.

Lighting wasn't grand; a gas mantle would dimly glow,

In the living room, but nowhere else, just candles to show

Us to the outside loo, or maybe, up the stairs to bed

But not up to the attic, because my older brother said,

'There are ghosts up those stairs;' I don't know how he knew

He hadn't seen them; he was scared to go up the attic too.
The war was over; bombs were gone; the lovely house we had
Was gone as well, and we were here, and times were really bad.

So, when you feel the pangs of hunger, what else can you do?
But steal some food, or other stuff, perhaps some money too?
So, we broke into a bakery, had a feast of cakes and cream
But very soon the police came by, and little did I dream,

I'd end up in a children's home, be taken from my mum,
They dragged me screaming from the court, she said: 'go with them son!'
I meekly marched out to the van; six years I would be there.
At least I got some food each day, and a brutal kind of care.

It housed a hundred other boys and any new recruits
Soon learned they had to fight like hell, to settle all disputes.
Fifty boys would make a circle, then we traded blow for blow,
It was a bruising bloody battle when the teacher shouted: 'go!'

And when the fights were ended, there's not a word would pass
The lips of any single boy, to do so would be crass -
A flogging with wire woven straps on bare buttocks; oh, the pain,
In front of all one hundred boys, you'd never speak again!

Winners were designated by the teacher, each time a fight took place

And if you disagreed with him, don't show it on your face!

No dumb insolence was tolerated, very little was, that's true.

When he said 'jump!' You jumped if you knew what's good for you.

The years have flown. I don't know how they've gone so fast and now

In my old age, when thinking back, I often wonder how.

The beatings and the floggings don't bring on thoughts of hate,

Instead, I pine and yearn to do it all again, for strangely, it was great.

So, you can no doubt gather that my childhood was extremely violent. During these early years, up until the age of sixteen, I had undergone rigorous training, including boxing, judo, weight training, and all aspects of keep fit programs at 'The School.'

This is a photograph of me at eighteen, a couple of years after being released from 'The School.'

Having gone through this meant that I was quite well-equipped to deal with any violence that came my way. Unfortunately, violence seemed to follow me, even to the point, where as a youth I was jailed for fighting when a boy attacked me, and I responded in the way that 'The School' had taught me so well. He was a much bigger, heavier-built boy who outweighed me by several stone, but he was quite badly injured and as a result, I was incarcerated for three months for Grievous Bodily Harm.

GBH is classed as a very serious crime and normally receives a sentence of three or four years, but it was conclusively proven by independent witnesses that the boy started it all off by attacking me from behind. Everyone said that was the reason the judge was so lenient; I was defending myself. At the time I thought my punishment was harsh as I saw myself as the innocent victim.

While attempting to squeeze my testicles, fortunately for me, (I thought), he missed the target and grabbed the end of my penis which became very badly bruised, but I was sure that I got away lightly, because, during the days that followed, I didn't notice any ill effects and very soon felt as they say, as right as rain.

Years later I married Jeannine, my wife of sixty years. She had auburn hair, and green eyes and was around five feet four inches tall; I thought she was lovely. We had six children; five boys and a girl. Many years later, I began to feel discomfort in my penis, it itched constantly, and over a period of a few years, the doctor prescribed different creams that eased the problem somewhat. As time wore on, this became more troublesome until finally I was referred to Mount Vernon Hospital for a biopsy and was diagnosed as benign. In my mind, I was convinced that they had diagnosed it wrong, and many months later, they said it was cancerous, and I had to have a course of Radiotherapy lasting a week. I found that very daunting and traumatic, and it left me in a very depressed state. Shortly after the treatment, the gland erupted and was excruciatingly painful and resembled a busted tomato. Jeannine wanted to have a look to see what the treatment had done for me. She cried when she saw it and said that she never would have believed me. Over a period of several months, it healed up and I was sure I had found peace of mind; I was cured.

Five years later I was feeling pretty awful; I had a dreadful bout of Flu,' and lost my sense of smell. I then developed a growth on the side of the gland again and I was referred back to the hospital. While this was going on, my sense of smell didn't return completely, and that convinced me there was a connection, and I was certain that the growth was cancerous.'

On the day of my appointment, a nurse fetched me from the waiting room, and the doctor who was at his desk studying my file looked up and said: 'Get undressed and get on that trolley.'

He started going over my abdomen very thoroughly, as I thought. he turned to the nurse and gestured at my penis: 'This is cancerous.' He said.

Then he resumed going over my abdomen but stopped again and said: 'It has spread to the lymph nodes too.'

He didn't talk to me or even seem to consider the fact that I was present, the whole thing was so cold and impersonal. I instantly remembered when my mother was operated on for a stomach ulcer, it was discovered she had cancer. I could hear my brother's voice saying: 'She's got cancer and secondary's all over her body.'

My God, I thought, '*Is this how it is to be with me too?*'

I sat by her bedside and watched her go from a woman in her early sixties to what appeared to be a woman of ninety; she was dead in just over a week.

I felt as though a death sentence had just been passed on me. I hoped that I would live long enough to see Christmas over, and then hopefully, my family would be spared that Christmas treat.

The doctor left the room, and the nurse took his place at the desk and studied my notes.

'You're very fortunate that the radiotherapy kept the cancer at bay for five years,' she said.

I was getting dressed and said: 'Uh, sorry, what?' Then I muttered, 'Small comfort now.'

Upon returning home I felt rather glum, and as I entered the living room, Jeannine appeared shocked. 'I'll call you back,' she said to the phone, and without taking her eyes off me, she set it down.

'What did they say?'

'They said I'm very lucky that the Radiotherapy kept cancer at bay for five years, but it is now definitely cancerous. It's not just my penis, the doctor says it has also spread to my lymph nodes and they are going to send me a date to go in for an operation.'

Jeannine wept.

I said, 'Can you get in touch with the children? I need all of them here. It's time to call a family meeting and bring this thing out into the open.'

The children already knew what was going on, but I had never discussed the problem with them, in fact, I had never discussed it with anyone. I desperately didn't want anyone to know. Jeannine called it my secret disease, but it felt so personal to me that I just couldn't talk about it; up until now.

The following evening, all our grown-up family, Danny, Seamus, Claire, Tom, Nathan, and David, were seated around the room and I said: 'I have asked you all to come here today because I have some rather disturbing news. When I was a boy of around twenty, I had a fight with a gypsy guy and he tried to squeeze my testicles, but he missed and ended up squeezing my penis. At the time, I thought I was lucky, but over the years it became problematic. About five years ago, I had to have radiotherapy on my penis. At the hospital yesterday, they said that I would need to have an operation because I now have penile cancer and it has spread to my lymph nodes. What I wanted to say to you was this: if it has spread to my lymph nodes, I will not be having an operation, I think that would just prolong the agony; the long-term prognosis for this is not good, so the time factor would be very brief. If that's the case, I feel sure I will be dead anyway and I might as well meet my maker as a complete man.'

Danny pointed at the others and said: 'If that is your decision, we will respect it.'

That actually made me cry, it was the seeming finality of it. In turn, they came forward and kissed me goodbye, I was very distressed and quietly wiped the tears from my eyes; Jeannine was sobbing.

It was the most miserable time in my life. We felt as though there was a black cloud looming over us. I would have no peace of mind and would not be able to face up to my decision until the results came through. I felt that this being my last Christmas, it should have been a happy time, but no, I just couldn't lift myself out of what seemed like a black hole. I was positive I was going to die and prepared myself mentally for such an event. *Well*, I thought, *if I die this week, it will save me the trouble of having to do it next week.*

A few days later Jeannine handed me a letter and upon opening it, with a look of disgust, I said: 'They've set the scan for the last week in January. For Christ's sake, I'll be dead by then!'

This was torturing her as well. She was suffering just as much as me, and it was also putting an immense strain on us financially. I was in such a state that I was unable to work, and the more time I had on my hands, the more depressed and worried I became. I talked it over with Jan and we decided to go to the Hospital. It didn't matter that I hadn't got an appointment. I remembered from way back when my mother was ill that there was a Lady Almoner. I was sure that she would be the one to see. She had of course been superseded by the new generation...a Social Worker. She was quite brisk and attentive and listened as I explained how I felt, and that I had been diagnosed as having penile cancer and it had spread to my lymph nodes.

'Would you mind waiting here?' She said and left the room. Upon her return, she said: 'There is someone coming to see you shortly.'

I was rather taken aback when the head Surgeon, a dark-haired quite attractive forty/fiftyish lady Surgeon, and the Registrar entered the room. She said that she had no idea that I was in such distress.

I said: 'I feel as though I have had a death sentence passed on me, and just dumped and left to get on with it. When I was examined, it shook me. I had no idea that I would be diagnosed as having cancer of the lymph nodes.'

She said: 'The Registrar will go right now to the Scanner and arrange an urgent appointment for you, okay?'

I nodded in agreement and they both got up and left.

'All right?' The Social Worker asked, and I nodded. 'You can wait here if you want, or you might as well go to the canteen and get a cup of coffee while you are waiting.'

I had just taken a bite of my sandwich when I spotted the Social Worker running towards me frantically waving her arms.

'Have you swallowed anything?' I shook my head.

'Spit it out! Don't swallow it!' Looking at Jeannine she said: 'They can take him right now as long as he hasn't had anything to eat or drink. You haven't drunk any coffee, have you?'

I looked up from the tissue that I was spitting into: 'No.'

'Well, that was lucky, wasn't it?' She said.

I went to the Outpatient Clinic on the pre-arranged day feeling all fluttery inside. The Registrar smiled and with a wave of his hand swept my worries away: 'The results say that the lymph nodes are clear, so that's a good thing.' Then his smile faded, 'Can we take a look?'

I stripped off and got on the examination table and he turned my penis in his hand, this way and that, squeezing it. As it was so painful, he didn't have to tell me that although the scan was clear, this was a problem.

He said, 'I'm sorry to say this is definitely cancerous!'

He scribed a diagonal line across the gland with his index finger and said that the malignant growth on the gland would be removed by taking part of the gland away. The complete removal of the gland didn't seem to be an option; he would conserve as much of the gland as possible.

'You will still be able to have normal sex you know,' he assured me.

Jeannine was present during the examination. She cried and said that she didn't need sex, she just wanted me to be well; sex was not important to her.

I felt so forlorn and dejected as I entered the ward on the day of the operation. Nil by mouth since the night before. While the nurse was taking my details, a very brisk and officious Sister approached.

She handed me a white gown. 'Come along my dear, take your clothes off and put this on and get into bed!'

A few minutes later she was back, 'I'm going to give you an injection, and when I do, you mustn't get out of bed, okay?'

I nodded, and she injected me in the buttock; I felt that this was the end and thought: *If I don't come out of the anesthetic they'll probably be doing me a favour.*

As we entered the operating theatre a nurse took my hand; everything was swimming.

'I'm the anesthetist,' she said and inserted a needle into a vein on the back of my hand. 'I want you to count to ten aloud.'

'One...two...three...'

I came to on the stretcher as it bumped over the risers in the doorway as it was leaving the operating theatre.

'I need to go to the toilet,' I told the nurse.

'Don't worry, just let it go, my dear, you've got a catheter with a bag.'

The operation was deemed a great success, completely eradicating cancer, but in the process, two and a half inches had been cut off my penis. In the period that followed, I attended regular check-ups and looking at this logically, I regarded it as a life-saving operation, and I even felt lucky to be alive; the black cloud was gone.

The lady surgeon approached me afterward and said: 'We are so delighted with the result of your operation; would you mind if we photographed you for our records?'

I agreed because my life had returned to some sort of normality. Contrary to what I thought prior to the operation when they kept telling me, 'You will be able to have normal sex.' At the time I just could not believe them, but it came about that I was able to have normal sex. I managed to get my mind around this and accept it, and on cancer? I even told Jeannine: 'I know I felt that they were really severe, especially when they previously said that they would conserve as much of the gland as possible, but this will never come back you know.' I was absolutely confident that I had been cured.

Chapter 2

I attended the clinic every three months or so for check-ups. During one of these routine checks, the examining doctor took the end of what was later to be termed as the 'neo foreskin,' and rolling it between his finger and thumb, he said: 'You have trouble going to the toilet.' There was no question mark on the end of it, he was telling me, not asking, and I thought: *I do spray a little.* But before I replied, he continued: 'You should come in and I will dilate this for you; do you know what that means?'

I shrugged and looked questioningly.

'It means passing an instrument up inside the urethra and expanding it so that you don't have a problem going to the toilet.'

'Do you think that's really necessary?' I asked.

'Of course! You will be in and out in one day! No problem, much better for you.'

I had great faith in this hospital, they had turned my whole life around. I pondered a moment and said: 'Okay, I'll be guided by you.'

Once again, a date was set up for me to go in.

No problem! Just a day visit, I thought as I entered the ward and was seen straight away by a petite, pretty little nurse who took all my details. I didn't have the horrible, dejected feeling that I felt when I had gone for the initial operation. Everything was quite calm and okay in my mind; *it's a simple dilatation,* I thought.

The nurse sat on the bed beside me as I was about to get undressed: 'We have to be sure we have got the right person, you know,' she said, smiling, 'Do you understand what's being done today?'

I rocked my hand to and fro, gesturing yes, no, yes, no. 'Yes, I do, dilation'

She smiled: 'Actually, it's dilatation! Dilatation of the urethra, that means passing an instrument up the tube towards the bladder and dilating or expanding it so that you don't have a problem passing water.'

'Yes,' I said, 'that's what I thought.'

About five minutes later, an Asian-looking gentleman turned up and said: 'Hello, I'm the anesthetist; I will be producing a sleep for you today.'

I told him I had a slight cold and he assured me that there would be no problem, but he would mention it to the surgeon anyway. I came round again as the trolley bumped over a door riser while leaving the Theatre.

'I need to go to the toilet,' I said, and then thought for a moment and said: 'Have I got a catheter in?'

'Yes.'

'Aw shit,' I moaned and thought that was very strange. I assumed that they had cut a blockage away in the tube so I had to have it in case of infection.

I was taken back to the ward knowing I was no longer a day patient.

A nurse took my temperature. 'Do you feel hot?'

'I feel as though I am being parboiled.' I said.

'Your temperature is very high.'

'Like what?'

'Thirty-nine.'

'How does that compare with ninety-eight point four? My brain doesn't work in this metric rubbish,' I said.

'I really don't know, but it's over a hundred.'

She gave me some tablets to stabilise it and I was soon back to normal, temperature-wise.

On the second day, I went to the bathroom and hung the catheter bag on the side of the bath. I tried having a look to see what had been done but there was nothing to see as I was so badly swollen. There was a considerable amount of blood crusted around the end that I tried unsuccessfully to wash off. On the third day, they removed the catheter and told me that I was to be discharged on Sunday, but before that, they would give me lessons in the use of the catheter. During that day, a group of doctors gathered at the end of the ward and having a discussion. They were just out of earshot, but I was certain they were discussing me and I feigned sleep even though I was watching them very intently. Several times in turn they gestured towards me.

Later on, a doctor, a tall dark man came to my bedside and said, 'Mister Bryans, I'm sorry to tell you, unfortunately, we haven't anyone spare to teach you the use of the catheter.'

I thought that was odd, even though I had no idea there was a problem. Later that day, I was more than a bit confused when, as I was being discharged, they handed me around twenty catheters and again I wondered why they had skipped teaching me the procedure.

A couple of days later, I was at home in the upstairs bathroom, trying to bathe it as the swelling had subsided a little. For the first time, I was able to see what had been done and was so shocked that I bellowed down to Jan.

'What is it? What's wrong?' She shouted back.

'They've cut the bloody thing off!' I howled.

In the days that followed she was really sympathetic and supportive. Words could never describe the anguish I felt when I realised what they had done. I could only imagine that this would be akin to severe shell shock. They had cut off over three-quarters of what was left from the initial operation. I was reduced from four and a half inches to less than an inch. I knew instantly that I would never be able to go to the toilet normally again, and sex? I knew that had gone forever as well. If I could have got my hands on the surgeon at that moment, I would have strangled the life out of him. There wasn't even enough of it to apply a dressing; it had been chopped off. There was no finesse in this operation, it was as though it had been whacked off with pruning shears. It was raw and completely flat at the end and wept continuously so that it fused to my underclothes sealing the urethra; it left me that I couldn't pass urine at all.

I dashed to the doctor as fast as I could and was seen almost immediately by my regular doctor. He was a man of average height and quite stocky with reddish hair. He seemed to be quite bored as he sat listening to my tale of woe; I even expected him to yawn, but he didn't.

'I suppose we'd best have a look,' he said rather impersonally as he rose and lounged on the side of his desk.

I agonised as I peeled my clothing off it and when it was exposed, it was raw and bright red. He brought both his hands to his mouth in shock and recoiled physically, cringing, he sucked his breath inward through clenched teeth.

'Ohhh!' he whispered, his voice quavering: 'My word that does look painful.'

'It is agony,' I moaned.

He prescribed a gel to numb it and a nozzle about as thick as a heavy knitting needle to pierce the urethra.

Back home, in the privacy of my bathroom, cringing in pain I gingerly applied some of the gel with a cotton ball and pierced the raw end. Even then it was so excruciatingly painful that I almost passed out. Because I had to do this every time I needed to go to the toilet. I was worried that there was a danger of the risk of infection. I lived with the pain during every waking hour as by the time I needed to toilet, my clothing had fused to the raw wound again. My nights were fraught with horrific nightmares about knives chopping, operations going wrong, waking up screaming and the sweats; how I hated the sweats, having to change my night clothes two or three times a night. It was as though someone had thrown a bucket of water over me. The pain that I had to endure inserting the nozzle each time was more than I could bear so I decided to try using the catheter which although harrowing, was very slightly less distressing. It was a little less in girth and kept the urine out of the open wound where it split with each use of the nozzle and felt as though it had been doused with salt. During this initial period, I wrote the following letter to the Hospital:

I was discharged from Hospital two days ago on Sunday 28th November. It is only now that the swelling has subsided that I realise just what has been done. I must say that I am very shocked and absolutely furious. When I visited the Outpatient Clinic on the 13th of September, I was examined by the Surgeon and he told me I was having problems passing water. I agree there was a problem, I felt as though there was some sort of restriction or perhaps the actual tube was stepped, a legacy from the operation last year. He said that the urethra had become restricted and needed dilating or 'stretched.' He explained in case I was not familiar with the term 'Dilating.'

He said he would arrange for me to come in and have that done. I agreed and went in on the 25th as a day patient. When the nurse was doing the preliminary checks, she asked me: 'Do you understand what is being done today?'

'I think so,' I replied.

'Dilating of the urethra,' she explained. 'That means passing an instrument up inside the tube towards the bladder and 'enlarging' or 'dilating' it. So that you don't have difficulty passing water.'

'Yes,' I said: 'that's what I understood.'

The realisation of what has taken place has just hit me like a thunderbolt. On close examination, I see that nothing of the kind took place. What did take place was, that the end has been chopped off as though with a meat cleaver. There had already been around fifty percent of the penis removed in the previous operation when I understood that *part of the gland would be saved, `if possible.' I accept that you must have felt that it was not possible or wise to conserve the gland as there would have been a risk of further infection. This has added insult to injury, especially when I know that this carvery was unnecessary; it did not need doing. Dilation, as explained to, and agreed by me, would have been perfectly adequate. I would never have agreed to what has been done. I feel as though I have been completely destroyed by this episode when I was in no position to defend myself. Whoever took the decision to do what was done was, in my opinion, uncaring and brutal and acted illegally. Would you kindly let me know what you are going to do about this `Blunder?'*

Yours sincerely

I was a bit worried about the content, so I went to the Citizens Advice Bureau and was seen by an elderly lady adviser who read my letter wide-eyed. Seeing the look on her face, I said: 'It is a bit of a horror story.'

'Absolutely!' She retorted. 'You must go to AVMA! 'Action for Victims of Medical Accidents,' it's a charity. They will advise you on what solicitor to engage. These solicitors have to be specialists in this field or they will be blown away in court.'

Physically, I was so badly affected and the mental stress of using the catheter was so unbearable that I returned to my doctor. He was quite insistent that I should be seen by the surgeon again. The hospital appointment arrived and it was for over four weeks' time. I was very worried about that so I paid him another visit and he was furious. 'They will see you a lot sooner than that or they'll have me to deal with,' he snapped angrily.

The appointment was brought forward to two days and I was seen by the lady surgeon and because I was in such a mess, she said: 'You will have to come in, in the morning!'

I was horrified and said: 'I can't do that!'

Her nostrils flared, displaying her anger: 'Are you refusing to come in?' She asked indignantly.

'No, I am not refusing,' I said, 'I have to get my mind around this, I am not ready yet, I am in a state of severe shock.'

Her attitude changed and she appeared to be really concerned about my welfare, 'I realise you are in shock; we have a lady at this hospital, a psychologist and she specialises in post-traumatic stress; I shall make an urgent appointment for you with her.'

She was absolutely insistent that I should attend the appointment.

Urgent appointments were set up, she was a pretty, slender, dark thirtyish lady, and upon entering her office she said: 'Everything we discuss here is in the strictest of confidence.' I immediately felt at ease.

'So where shall we start? Shall we go back to your childhood?'

I thought that was odd; she wanted to delve into my childhood, how deprived I had been, my schooling at the 'approved' school, my violent youth and how I had been jailed for fighting. I had long since put all of that behind me, it was like a distant memory. Over forty years had elapsed and I really didn't see the relevance, so, because of that, after the second visit I stopped going. Even though she was based at the very same hospital as the lady surgeon and she *was* her preferred choice, at the time, I never dreamt that her findings would be used as a weapon against me. When the case came to court all of this so called 'strictest of confidence' stuff suddenly became very conveniently in the public domain, and they described me as being the product of an approved school, a street fighter and from a very dubious background, most of which I had to agree with as my early days certainly left a lot to be desired, but in the years since our marriage, my wife and I had fostered countless children and adopted four others, three of whom were 'very special needs!' Of course, none of that was referred to when they were ditching the dirt. I thought that all of what was said regarding this in court was totally irrelevant to the case in hand and was being used to paint a picture of me in the worst possible light and blacken my character.

Because we had adopted four children, they inferred that I was extremely fit and well, otherwise I would not be able to undertake such a monumental, physically and mentally taxing task as fostering. The other side of the problem for me was; if I was to be considered 'unfit for work,' that would raise a question mark over my ability to care for foster children and we would lose even that meagre income also, and leave us with nothing.

Any of you who have had a catheter inserted might have found this painful or distressing. For the uninitiated, it means inserting a plastic tube up inside the urethra until it reaches the bladder, at which point the urine runs freely away. It brought to mind the first time I had a catheter inserted and a rather sickly-looking bearded patient asked me: 'Ever had one of those in before mate?'

'No,' I said.

'Huh, huh!' He gave a mirthless laugh: 'You'll know all about it when they take that bastard out, it's like pissing broken bottles!'

The scar tissue on the end where it had been 'chopped off,' continued to close in, even after the so-called corrective dilatation that they arranged and within a couple of weeks, I was back using the catheter again, although not quite as frequently as before; two to three times a week. The problem was, if I left it more than two or three days, the end would fuse together again and become so tight, that it would split and bleed even with the catheter. This additional distress was something that I very quickly learned to avoid, as it greatly increased the pain when using it, especially if urine got into the open wounds.

Over the years that followed, this was an extremely harrowing and debilitating chore that became almost imperceptibly, progressively worse. The time between each use of the catheter diminished very slightly. I invariably had urine infections, scorching pains, and blood cells in the urine, and with all of this, my resistance was lowered so that I was subsequently subject to chest, ear, and in fact many infections not seemingly related. So much so that I said to my long-suffering wife, 'This lot is going to see me off!' And prior to all of this, I was a man who was very rarely ill.

As they had photographed my penis after the successful operation, I just knew that it was vital that I get photographs at the early stage of this latest development. I scanned the yellow pages and found a photographer specialising in insurance claims.

'Hmmm,' I cleared my throat when he asked what sort of photos I needed.

'Well actually, I need you to photograph my penis!'

He spluttered on the end of the line: 'That's a first!'

'If you don't want to do it -' he cut me off.

'Oh, I'll do it!' He assured me, 'It's just that, well -'

'I understand perfectly,' I said, 'it's certainly not easy for me either.'

So, it was agreed and I went and had some more photos taken. I now had a full set of before and after and they were strikingly different. It was unfortunate that around six weeks had elapsed before I had the photos taken, so there had been time for it to heal somewhat and the end that had been completely flat had swollen and taken on a slightly domed shape. It didn't really show it in its worst state, even though I was still in extreme pain all the time.

I never received a single reply to any of my letters to the hospital. After a few months, on the directions of AVMA, I finally ended up with a London firm who were supposedly '*the*' specialists in this field. I was summoned to the Solicitor's office where I was briefed by the solicitor dealing with my case and he went over everything. He informed me that my operation had been carried out by Mister Thomas, a Locum, who had left the country and gone back home to Australia. I felt quite at ease with my solicitor, he was a tall smartly dressed fair-haired young man who came over as very experienced and efficient.

Because I felt so angry, I said: 'Do you think I'll get enough out of this case to go to Australia and kill this son of a bitch?'

He smiled, assuming I was joking, and said: 'My boy, you'll get enough out of this to hire a hit man to do it for you, this is a huge claim, and we are very confident here. You see these surgeons come over here to learn how to cut because they're not allowed to do it in their own country, for if they did, they would be roasted!'

At this point, I was still going through the Legal Aid channels but hadn't had the final decision, so I told him that in the event of not getting Legal Aid, I could raise money on our property.

'I would **not** recommend anyone going down that road!' he said vehemently. 'You will meet a stone wall of resistance and when you have lost your property, you will then have to back out! However, you will get Legal Aid!'

A meeting was set up at the Barrister's office. I knocked on the door and my solicitor ushered me to a chair. The office just oozed opulence and he pointed at a portly, middle-aged, slightly unshaven man seated to one side and said: 'Jim, this is your team of experts. Mister Short here is a surgeon, he's our medical expert, and this is Mister David our barrister, he is your legal expert. So, if you could just briefly outline for them what took place.'

I said: 'Okay. I went in for dilatation, a small operation during which, while I was out cold, the surgeon cut my penis off, leaving me with a stump less than an inch long. The hospital, lying bastards that they are, are denying it, saying it was a simple circumcision. Prior to this, I had a very successful operation for penile cancer. The head surgeon, a lady, was so pleased with the result that she asked me if they could photograph my penis for their records, and I agreed. However, after this total balls up, I knew I needed more photos, so I recently contacted a professional photographer and had these taken.'

I handed them to Mister Short and said: 'See what you think!'

He studied them briefly, then as he passed them to Mister David, he said: 'But this is a gentleman, and you're calling him a liar.'

I was quite shocked and said: 'No I'm not! I'm calling him a fucking liar! And if he was in this room right now, I would strangle the life out of the bastard!'

Mister David jumped to his feet and leaning forward on his desk he said: 'My goodness Mister Bryans! I think you are suffering from severe stress.'

I glanced at him for a few seconds and Mister Short intervening said: 'It's difficult to make a decision; these photographs are quite different to what the hospital is saying.'

'Huh! I would say so!' I retorted.

I turned to Mister David and said: 'What I think I am suffering is something akin to severe shell shock. For goodness sake, I've had my penis chopped off. I am using a catheter three times a week and will be for the foreseeable future! When I went for my check-up, their new plastic surgeon examined me and said: 'I can do absolutely nothing for you, Mister Bryans.'

I took a long hard look at my medical expert; I had reservations about him. He was well into middle age, complete with middle age spread, and slightly unshaven. This so-called team didn't exactly bolster my confidence. A few weeks later, my solicitor sacked the barrister and I asked, why?

'He didn't measure up.' He replied.

I didn't say it, but I thought: 'I hope you sack my medical expert too because I reckon he doesn't measure up either!' Needless to say, they didn't.

For seven years after the incident, I met a stone wall of resistance from the hospital, where they told my solicitor, 'It was a simple circumcision,' or 'it was just a little bit of skin.' This response came only after many months, where previously they drew ranks and said absolutely nothing. My solicitor informed me that when an operation is performed and they cut anything away, the section that is cut away has to be preserved. He instructed me to ask for the following, and I quote from my letter to the head surgeon:

You also told me that the piece of skin had been sent to the lab for tests and had come back negative. Would you please also let Mrs. Charles have copies of:

The Lab tests

The Pathology tests

Histology

To my knowledge, we never got any of these, and the (piece of skin)? According to my solicitor, it was (very conveniently) mislaid.

The very ones who should have been looking after my welfare were bound together in opposition, presumably because I was suing them, and rightly so in my estimation! Any replies to letters were never with me, only with my solicitor, who incidentally had now changed as the original one had left. My new solicitor was a middle-aged, nondescript man and I asked him: 'How much do you think a case like this would be awarded?'

'Over a hundred thousand!' He then rocked his head from side to side and said: 'Perhaps not two, but at least one.'

It was a sad day for me when this solicitor also left and I had yet another new one. He was a mid-thirties man, tall and slim with a huge mop of unkempt reddish, wavy hair. I thought he looked more like a hippy than a solicitor. Again, I was asked to come to the office, and again we went over the very same ground that the previous two had. Same questions and same answers. I asked him what he thought the possible outcome would be and he said: 'This will not make you a rich man Jim, so don't think you will be coming away with pots of money. You'll be lucky if you get twenty thousand. They might even offer you an out-of-court settlement.'

'If it's for less than a hundred and twenty thousand they can forget it!' I snapped.

From the outset, he assured me he would win my case. I never doubted that he would. Even though he came over as quite thorough, his goal and mine were leagues apart. He wanted and would be satisfied with what he classed as a win, but I wanted the best result. The thing that riled me was: no matter what the outcome would be, his payment was guaranteed. The opposition would pay his bill, or if the case collapsed then I would have to foot his bill if Legal Aid didn't. I was entirely dependent on his tenacity and determination but found him sadly lacking to the point of being utterly useless. I thought that my medical expert was also in a similar vein. I was stunned when he said that it was difficult to make a judgement.

I had the before and after photos and the end result that he could check at any time. I wondered just where the theatre staff was in all of this, there was never any mention of them, as though they were shrouded in a cloak of secrecy, or didn't even exist.

I was summoned to the solicitor's office again, to go through my medical records as he had now acquired a copy. As we were going through them, page by page, he exclaimed: 'Oh! There's a page missing here!'

It was the very appointment when my doctor had seen me on emergency, during which he had recoiled and gasped: 'My word that does look painful!'

I was shocked and angry, I wanted to sue him as well. I thought that could very possibly be vital evidence, especially when I'd had a follow-up visit and said that I was in litigation over the trouble with my penis.

I said, 'Do you remember when you examined me?'

He put his fingers to his lips and looking a bit wistful, whispered: 'Oh, I really don't recall that.'

'What the hell is this load of crap?' I retorted sarcastically, 'The old school tie?'

I knew he felt uncomfortable when he didn't reply, but studied his notes. It made me think that everyone in the health service had to be in collusion when a member of the public challenges them, and that was such a bitter pill to take as I had always held them in such high regard. I'd had a botched operation, followed by denials, and now this. I was livid and pressed my solicitor for action.

He said: 'Now Jim, there is nothing to be gained by going down that road.' I found that odd as I thought it might help to highlight just what goes on in a case like this.

We differed greatly and not just about that and I wrote a quite vehement letter to him as follows:

Dear David, 24th November 1997

To say things have been on my mind is probably the understatement of the year. When I first started the business of a claim, I thought that there was a chance I would not be granted Legal Aid, but I was quite determined to pursue this, and I saw an advertisement in a National Daily. 'Have you had an accident? No win, no fee.'

I got in touch with these people and told one of them my circumstances and what had happened. His exact words were; 'This will be a huge claim.' However, he assured me that I would most certainly get Legal Aid, but in the event of being refused, do not hesitate to get in touch. This seems to be in stark contrast to the attitude I am getting from you. When this is over, you will get your money, no matter what. I however have to rely on your vigour and determination in this matter. The fact that there was a page missing in my medical files from my Doctor, I know this to be true because there isn't even a note of the medication he prescribed on the day I attended surgery when I was unable to go to the toilet. I am also sure that he would have noted my condition as he recoiled in shock when he examined me. It seems to me that this is being disregarded completely or deemed to be of no importance. I thought that this could very well be vital evidence. I am being told, 'You will get some money, not a lot, it certainly won't make you a rich man, and Mister Thomas will still be practicing surgery.'

The figure you suggested is probably around £20,000.00

You know that I have been in financial difficulties and because of this, I went and spoke to my Bank Manager whom I know quite well. This was before any discussion I had with you about money. I told him of my predicament and that my solicitor, Peter B-------, had said that as this was a unique case, I would probably only get about a hundred thousand off them. My Bank Manager was quite shocked. 'Is that all,' he said 'that's a paltry figure for that. Why you couldn't even be a member of a golf club. If you went for a shower you would be held up to ridicule.' And I have to say that I absolutely agree with his comments. I can't help thinking that if your returns were dependent on your efforts, in other words, if only a percentage of what was forthcoming was yours, would any stone be left unturned? I think not! Incidentally, I am writing this letter in the middle of the night. I.e. 4.30 am

Yours sincerely etc.

However, he assured me that the plastic surgeon they had located could do a 'rebuild.' So, when I was having one of my usual check-ups that were supposedly post-operative care, on this occasion, I was seen by their brand-new plastic surgeon who actually examined me, and that was a very rare event. Normally, it was as though they didn't want to see this 'problem,' and not even have a look but ask: 'Still using the catheter?'

'Yes!' I would snap angrily. The longer this went on, the more I felt this seething hatred build up because of what I saw as their continuing negligence.

They didn't seem shocked, or decide to arrange treatment to resolve what I'm sure they knew was a serious problem, their usual reply was: 'Oh! You must be something of an expert at that now.'

My solicitor told me that when I am examined by their plastic surgeon, ask to be referred to Mister Braka, the plastic surgeon he had located, and when I did, he retorted: 'We can't do that! That would cost the Trust money!' It was as though I shouldn't have asked in the first place. This was after five years of using the catheter three times a week and by this time I was facing the daunting prospect of it nearing four times a week. The alternative they offered was that I should come in every six months for dilatation. I was sure their ulterior motive was: the fact that they offered, would probably look good on their records when the case came up.

How would a judge know that this extremely distressing treatment was useless for me? Two days after the original botched operation, when I was taken in for emergency dilatation, I had to revert to the use of the catheter in less than two weeks. I was sure that their recommendation would not have benefitted me, it would have created more stress and discomfort, and that was why I refused.

However, apart from that reason, the thought of them performing surgery on me again just filled me with revulsion! I hated and distrusted them so much so that when I was confiding in Doug, an old and trusted friend, I said: 'I'd sooner go through the gates of hell than have those bastards perform surgery on me again!'

At one point, because of what I saw as their continued negligence, I said to my solicitor: 'I'm not even going to go and see these bastards!'

He said: 'Oh yes you will, because if you don't, it will be used against you when this case comes to court!'

My doubts and fears were well founded when I discovered that, entered into my records, someone had written, and I quote: 'progressively poor stream and spraying and hesitancy.' They also put a note to say that I'd had two courses of radiotherapy, which I did not! At no time did I ever mention stream to them. The time that this entry referred to was prior to the original botched operation and at that point my stream was very good, my problem was the direction it took! They also claimed to have given me lessons on the use of the catheter, but my aftercare was zero. Notes were also entered in on several following check-ups: 'Stream is poor.' I wondered just how they would know anything about my stream, except to hazard a guess; I was using the catheter and most of the time, I didn't even have a stream! I never entered into conversation of any sort with them except on the one occasion, when the original Doctor who examined me and said: 'You should come in and I will dilate this for you.' He happened to be dealing with one of my check-ups and immediately upon recognition, I snapped angrily: 'Was it you who did my operation?'

He became very flustered and quickly denied it. Shaking his hands defensively in front of him he said: 'No, no! It wasn't me, I didn't do it!'

He then studied his paperwork and without looking up, asked: 'Still using the catheter?'

'Yes!' I snarled.

'Very well, we'll see you in six months!' He said and I knew he was glad to see the back of me.

Chapter 3

With the hospital's refusal and feeling that my doctor was now part of what I saw as a conspiracy, I dreaded having to ask him to refer me to Mister Braka. In fact, I absolutely hated the thought of setting eyes on him again, but I was determined to go. For some reason unknown to me, I was switched to a lady Doctor, Doctor Jaffe. She was a rather petite, dark, quite beautiful lady. As it turned out, this was a very fortunate turn of events. She was new to the practice and when I asked her to refer me, I got the impression that she was quite nervous and very apprehensive at the prospect. But I have to say that I was and still am, delighted with the effort she put in. She came through for me; I can't praise her too highly. She gave me the sympathy and understanding that I found, not lacking but non-existent at the hospital and got me referred to the specialist.

I went to Wordsley Hospital in the West Midlands, armed with my before and after photographs. I wanted to show this Mister Braka just what they had done! You could have knocked me over with a feather when he glanced at them and tossed them to one side and said: 'Both these photos have got BXO, I would recognise it anywhere! You had radiotherapy, didn't you?'

I answered a shocked, 'Err, yes.'

'We don't do that here, that's old hat!' He said. 'BXO (Balanitis Xerotica Obliterans) can be brought on by radiotherapy. It can damage the tissue and I'm afraid,' he gestured at the stump of my penis and said, 'All that has to go!'

I knew instantly what he was talking about. After the first operation, I was certain that the cancer had been successfully eliminated and I told Jeannine: 'This will never come back.'

But it didn't feel quite normal. The outer skin on my penis itched and had a shiny plastic feel and appearance to it, they prescribed several different creams, and I thought it was just a teething problem, so that was okay.

He pointed at the couch: 'Let's have a look then!'

After a very brief examination, he said: 'You are an urgent case, you need to come in as soon as possible!'

I immediately got the jitters and mumbled: 'I would like to talk this over with my wife first.'

His words were ringing in my ears: 'All that has to go!'

'Well,' he said, 'I wouldn't defer this if I were you, because the next thing I will hear is that you are brought in on an emergency; BXO will see to that! And if you refuse now, you might not get another chance.'

I was struck dumb. I knew what he was saying was true because on a daily basis, the torment was harder to bear, and the time between each use of the catheter had diminished.

'Right then!' He said: 'What I shall do is this. I shall put the wheels in motion; we'll make a date and you can cancel right up to the operation, that will give you plenty of time to think about it.'

I asked, 'How much is all of this going to cost?'

'Huh!' He retorted, 'It won't cost you a penny, it will all be done on the National Health!'

I was given a date within a matter of weeks, this being a time when most people were waiting many months. I couldn't help thinking, 'If I am such an urgent case, why did the other hospital not act accordingly?'

Due to my treatment there, I had built up such fear and suspicion of the medical profession that I was convinced I would be coming back from the Midlands in a box, but despite these fears, I was compelled to go. I just knew he was right; I *would* be brought in on an emergency and if I ended up in Mount

Vernon, it would be a one-way ticket; a complete removal! The mere thought of them performing emergency surgery on me, filled me with such horror, that if it became a prospect, I would probably jump off a bridge! At least this way, I thought I had a chance. I went into Wordsley Hospital the day before my sixty-second birthday, 18ᵗʰ June 1998, and they did a rebuild on my penis the next day, on my birthday would you believe?

I never dreamt that this would be such a lengthy operation and recovery or be so excruciatingly painful. The pain was something of a double whammy because they took a large section of skin, an area around the size of a house brick, off my thigh to do the rebuild and that was also very painful and took a long time to heal.

As it turned out, it was one of, if not the best decision of my life. The treatment I received at Wordsley was wonderful and in my opinion, it is a shining example of what an NHS hospital should be. I was transformed from a nothing back into a man. That was how I saw myself; I wasn't a man, and I most certainly wasn't a woman! I was a nothing! I thought then and still think that the surgeon was a genius and a credit to his profession. On my last visit to him I said: 'Many thanks for all you have done for me, I am forever in your debt.'

When I had the rebuild, the itching, the pain, and the discomfort disappeared; it eradicated all the problems Mount Vernon left me with and I have never had to use the catheter since! However, before I went in for the op, Mount Vernon insisted that I see their medical expert and their appointed psychiatrist. Their medical expert said: 'The reason he can't have sex is:' it's all in his mind.' Their psychiatrist said: 'There is absolutely nothing wrong with him, he's just angry.' Take a look at the before and after photographs and see if you think I just imagined it and it was all in my mind!

This photo was taken by the Hospital after my first (successful) operation after it was reduced by two and a half inches

Photo 1

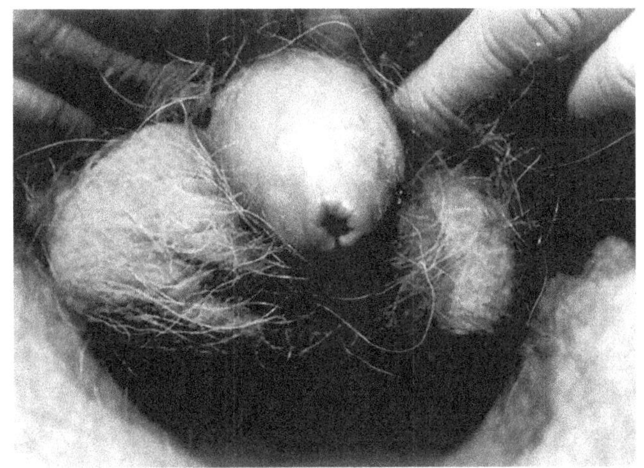

This one was taken privately by the photographer I engaged over six weeks after the botched surgery.

Photo2

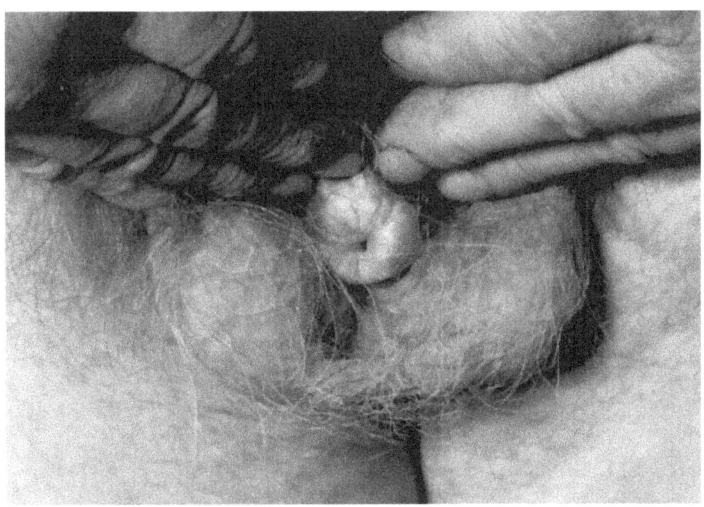

The fact that they said it was all in my mind, made me think: *Could this possibly be interpreted by the court that my mind was disturbed?* Which of course it was! And *could that have an effect on the outcome in my favour?*

Almost immediately, they appointed another medical expert who came up with a different prognosis. I told my solicitor about BXO and how I feared that my case would collapse, but it didn't. All the other doctors, including my medical expert, said: 'Of course he hasn't got BXO!' And I thought, 'I wonder if they are still using Radio Therapy?'

So, do I believe the genius who cured me in two weeks, or the ones that neither gave nor offered remedial surgery for over five years? I think I know the answer to that one, but you will have to come to your own conclusion. However, if their performance to date was anything to go by, all these years later, I think if it had been left to them, I would more than likely still be using the catheter; even now!'

When the case got close, my solicitor said that they had lodged eight thousand pounds in the court and he said: 'Now, you don't have to accept this, but if you don't and you are awarded less, then you will have to pay all their costs from that date, which could amount to a figure in excess of twenty thousand pounds.'

Do I have to say that I found his whole attitude and his demeanour absolutely useless, I felt that he regarded me purely as his meal ticket.

I retorted: 'I don't give a damn how much they lodge; go for it!'

At this point Jeannine who was war weary sighed: 'Oh Jim, all I want is for this to end!'

I knew they were playing mind games, that enraged me and made me more determined than ever.

I told my solicitor: 'If I don't get fair treatment here, I will put it all on the internet! I'll tell the whole world just what happened here!'

I asked him: 'Have they located this Mister Thomas who did the operation?'

'Yes, they have,' he said, 'I'm afraid he will not be recalled, as far as we know, he is not a well man, by all accounts he has had a nervous breakdown.'

'Well!' I snapped, 'doesn't that just inspire confidence in you? I wonder how many other victims he left in his wake. He'd have had more than a nervous breakdown if I'd got my hands on him!'

My solicitor said he was going to investigate other similar cases to see what sort of award they had received and guess what? There isn't one! There has never been another case the same as mine; I am unique! What he did find out was that a lot of men lose their penis through penile cancer or accidents such as car crashes, dog, or even woman attacks. Recalling the case of: http://en.wikipedia.org/wiki/John_and_Lorena_Bobbitt.

During the court case, our medical expert was asked: 'What happens to these men?'

'A good many of them commit suicide,' he replied.

Now that I could understand, if I hadn't had my wife and family behind me, I think I would have more than likely joined them.

During a phone call, my solicitor said that he had spoken to the opposition and they had asked him how much he thought this case was worth.

'So?' I said.

'Between forty and fifty thousand,' he said.

I couldn't believe my ears. 'You did what?' I screamed. 'You had no right to do that! You have given them a ballpark figure, you had absolutely no right!'

I was so angry that I slammed the phone down on him; he didn't ring back!

When I first applied to these solicitors, they sent me a letter stating their terms and conditions, and one of the first rules was: 'You have to tell us what you want us to do.' I made it absolutely clear to all three solicitors, time and time again, that I felt my claim should be over one hundred thousand, as both previous solicitors had assured me. I felt as though I had Clive Burgess or Donald Maclean on my side and the opposition just had to be jumping up and down, rubbing their hands with glee. Was he getting a backhander from them? I just couldn't erase the thought from my mind!

During the run-up to the case, The Daily Mail did a very sympathetic article and when they interviewed my solicitor, he decided to up the amount; was it because of my reaction? I thought so.

'We shall be asking for in excess of sixty thousand,' he said.

I was outraged and felt that he had very successfully engineered a paltry award for me, and how I hated him for it!

He said: 'But Jim, these judges have criteria by which they work.'

'They most certainly do not!' I retorted. 'There has never been another case the same as mine! Both your predecessors assured me my case is unique and worth over a hundred thousand pounds!'

Well, if they didn't know before he blabbed his mouth off publicly to everyone, they certainly did now. I knew that having this figure made public, it was very simple mathematics; if you ask for sixty you are not going to get a hundred, or two hundred; fifty perhaps if you're lucky, and that was precisely how things transpired. I felt that a potentially high-profile case had been trivialised by my defence, and he had even said himself that my case was unique.

The very week after my case finished, a man was awarded six hundred thousand because he was afraid of black people; I was disgusted! I wondered, just what is the price of trauma? Seven years of sleepless nights or sweating it out through constant recurring nightmares. This was a twenty-four-hour-a-day thing that I knew wasn't going to disappear after the trial. If it had happened in America, I would possibly have been awarded ten or even twenty times what I received here.

We arrived at court and while we were waiting in the lobby, my solicitor said: 'They will possibly make you an offer for an out-of-court settlement before we go in.'

I wondered if they would but said: 'I don't give a damn what they offer, I am going in any way!'

I felt in my heart of hearts that my case had been very effectively 'dashed,' by the very one defending me. In any case, they didn't make an offer. At this point, my barrister forewarned me that they would ask me if I thought that they had cut away the shaft. 'If you say that they have, I am warning you, this case will collapse.'

Although I found that absolutely disgusting, I did take note. It also reinforced my opinion that my team was rubbish! When we entered and were awaiting the Judge, the opposition's barrister approached a lady; an executive-looking type, and Jeannine overheard him whisper: 'This will very possibly hit the national press, are you sure you wish to proceed?'

To which she retorted through clenched teeth a very positive, 'Yes!'

They were determined to hold me up to public scrutiny and ridicule!

The first thing their barrister said was: 'Mr Bryans, I am going to ask you some very personal questions, but before I do, the Trust wishes me to convey their sincere apologies for this unnecessary procedure.'

'What hypocrisy,' I thought. 'Seven years of denial and now this?'

Then the first question came: 'Mr. Bryans, it is your opinion is it not, that the shaft of your penis was cut away?'

I said, 'All I know is that I went for a simple dilatation and went into the theatre with a normal working penis four and a half inches in length, and came out with a one-inch stump. Be it shaft, skin, or whatever, I am not a doctor. If you want to know the answer to that question, ask a doctor!'

I found the court case extremely distressing. When it was over, the Judge retired to make his decision and we waited in a lobby. My solicitor came and told me that judgement had been passed – 'Thirty-five thousand, plus expenses, plus interest, amounting to just under fifty thousand.' It didn't even pay off our accumulated debts that had mounted up over the seven years.

'It is a good result,' he said; I was livid!

This massive trauma that my wife and I had endured and I will continue to do so for the rest of my life, had been trivialised.

'I know the amount is derisory, but it is a good result.' He repeated.

Again, I wondered if he was working for both sides. That was the only thing that made sense to me. On the other hand, he may have been acting like a smart Alec at my expense; I suppose I will never know. At this juncture, I wondered how much the Judge valued his penis; not a lot I guess, when I considered the paltry sum awarded. I suppose I can't blame the Judge however, he had to work with the evidence presented to him.

It never occurred to me at the outset, but later on, I figured that any court case pursued by a member of the public against a Trust such as this is doomed to failure. People might win their cases, but the outcome is usually predetermined by 'top ranking,' defence lawyers, barristers, psychiatrists, and doctors, paid for by Trusts on an open cheque-book, and if they don't measure up, they are replaced, ensuring very successfully that the victims do not get the money! Legal Aid on the other hand holds the purse strings and as I see it, whether intentionally or not, puts the victim at the other end of the scale, as they are on limited spending. In my case, had I been in charge of finance, I would have sacked not only the barrister but also my third solicitor and my medical expert as well, although the more I thought about it, I began to realise why my original doctor probably tore the page out of my records. He didn't want to be involved, and my medical expert, despite the undisputable evidence of the photographs, was not just hesitant, but in my opinion, completely failed to act upon such evidence. After the court case was over, I would very likely be compensated and go home, but they, on the other hand, would have to return to normal work station and would be dealing with Trusts, where they would very possibly be ostracised by the Trusts and their colleagues, for their treachery in dealing with the opposition. So, I suppose I couldn't really blame them either, they could also meet the stone wall of resistance!

At the time, however, I felt that all three were not up to par and I thought that the final judgement justified my doubts. I also thought that Legal Aid was the very reason my solicitors kept chopping and changing; they were purely Legal Aid and of course, again, it holds the purse strings. So, later on, when I contacted my solicitors, I discovered that David had also gone, in search of greener pastures no doubt. It would be interesting to know if he upgraded to the opposition's solicitors or one of their affiliates.

For their statutory charge, my solicitors deducted something in the region of five thousand pounds and I wondered if I was charged in triplicate owing to the changes to the three different solicitors, because each time they did, we had gone back to square one! In the very brief period while I was awaiting confirmation on 'Legal Aid,' I received a letter from them saying that up until I was granted Legal Aid, the amount owing was £750.53. So, when they deducted five thousand pounds, it seemed to me as though solicitors like to be paid by both parties. After all, I did win my case! Or so they said, and when you win, surely the opposition pays the costs; don't they? Anyway, I should think it is safe to say that the charges from all the participants during the years that followed me getting Legal Aid, would have outstripped my award manyfold.

It did hit the national press, some of whom treated it as a joke and made what they thought were funny little quips.

'The Sun,' 'Hospital stumps up £50,000 for 1-in Willy.'

'The Mirror' '£50k for 'sex chop.'

Perhaps that is why I have always referred to them as the 'Beano' and the 'Dandy.'

If they had thought for a few moments about the pain and misery involved, they wouldn't think of it as a joke. They were however all in agreement that I had won my case, but I thought and still think that I was just fobbed off with pittance! When I read the Judgement, the Judge referred to other similar cases and talked of trifling amounts. Anyway, losing one's penis in, for example, a car accident, although the result is the same, it is to my mind very different from having someone whack it off unnecessarily when you are unconscious on an operating table, and then add insult to injury by denying it for seven years.

Chapter 4

Due to the press coverage, I was approached and took part in a TV program called 'Hospital Stories from Hell,' which was screened on a weekend.

The following week, my very good friend next door phoned and said: 'Jim, they've just had a phone-in program on the radio, and it was to vote for their 'Hero of the Week' and guess what? Nearly everyone voted for you.'

'Well, what do you know?' I said and thought: 'Yes! I did do the right thing.'

Later on, the producer of the TV Program phoned and asked me what I thought. Having seen the pain and anguish of the other participants and the paltry awards that they received with some of them even losing their property in the process, I said: 'So long as judges hand out parsimonious amounts, Trusts, whether in the right or wrong, will fight tooth and nail to the bitter end for that very reason; it pays them to. It's not the victim who gets the money; it's the lawyers, the barristers, and even the judges. It wouldn't surprise me if their costs in my case exceeded four or five times my award, each.'

'I know,' she said, 'And I know this doesn't help you, but the law has changed. They have to settle out of court now, they're not allowed to defend the indefensible anymore.'

While I was making the film, the producer asked me: 'Why would you want to do this?'

I said, 'Initially, I didn't want anyone to know; it was a very personal, private thing. Somehow, I felt ashamed, and I didn't even know why that should be, but as time went by, with their denials and fobbing off, I got the bit in my teeth and my shame turned to anger and I said: 'I'm going to fight you bloody lot!' And fight me they did, right to the final bell!

However, even now, all these years later, I am still seething with anger and I still want the whole world to know just what happened. I don't feel ashamed anymore, I did nothing wrong. I can walk down the street and look anyone in the eye!

A short time ago, because of the title, I watched a program called: '99 Most Bizarre Surgical Screw ups,' and I was surprised, but I have to say not shocked when I found that I was featured in it and was the very top of the list; number 99! My case was described as the most bizarre surgical screw-up of them all.

I also recently found this link:

BBC News | Health | £49,000 for bungled genital operation

http://news.bbc.co.uk/2/hi/health/273481.stm

Feb 5, 1999 ...

A man has won £49000 compensation from a hospital that removed most of his penis in a routine operation.

I was discussing the case with Jeannine and said: 'You know what? When the head surgeon insisted that I see her psychiatrist, I thought she was concerned, but I'm sure it was really to get some information that could be used for their defense, and didn't they make the most of it? The fact that we fostered countless children for years and adopted four, three of whom had 'special needs' wasn't even mentioned by our so-called team. If I'd had the opposition's team, we'd be sitting pretty now.'

I was famous! They had very successfully held me up to public ridicule, and on the cold February morning following the press release, there, scratched in the ice on the bonnet of my car was: 'Call me for sex, ha! Ha!'

Oddly enough that didn't bother me at all, but I had to laugh when Doug, my old friend phoned and I told him. He said: 'Don't worry about that Jim, the bastards are just jealous because they haven't got a dick worth fifty grand.'

Anyway, I think that no amount of money could ever have compensated me, or my wife and family for this disastrous botch up, or more importantly the trauma of the denials that followed. But, if I had been awarded what I considered to be a fair settlement, I would have shut up and there would have been nothing more about it. I'm sure they don't welcome adverse publicity and I hope that is food for thought for them; if it is not, it should be!

The strange thing is, it didn't end there. A week after the result of the court case was published in the press, the phone rang and a man's voice whispered. 'Are you the gentleman that was in the papers last week? Please don't put the phone down!'

'Don't worry, I'm not going to put it down!' I assured him.

'I'm in litigation with the same Trust that you were, I had my penis chopped off too.'

We had a chat on the phone and for convenience's sake, I shall call him Ray. He came to visit us on the Saturday and brought with him a ream of paperwork. He looked at me then at Jan and said: 'You're lucky, you've got her! My missus left me! I suppose I can't blame her; I'm evil you know, I'm so angry all the time, I feel like burning the bloody hospital down.'

'I know exactly what you mean,' I said, 'I feel rage all the time.'

'I can't believe the award that you got, fifty grand: that's pathetic! I want half a million for mine. He said as he rifled through his paperwork. 'I'm going to sue them because they gave me radiotherapy.'

'What?' I asked, clearly puzzled, 'I had radiotherapy.'

'Well, radiotherapy is a treatment that, in a good many cases, is responsible for the problem returning within five years. Did yours return in five years?'

'Yes, it did!'

'Did they offer you Brachytherapy?'

'Never heard of it, what is it?'

'Brachytherapy is renowned for virtually one hundred percent success in the treatment of penile cancer, invariably it does not return. Are you aware that when you were having radiotherapy, maybe even in the next room, there was a doctor who could have administered Brachytherapy and you would have very possibly been spared all your problems?'

'Christ!' I gasped. 'What, at Mount Vernon?'

'Yes! At Mount Vernon and I'll tell you better than that, it was pioneered at Mount Vernon by Doctor P. J. Hoskin!'

'What?' I exclaimed in disbelief.

'Sue them again!' He said.

'I can't, it's been over three years.'

'Yes, you can,' he said, 'Your time starts from the date of knowledge, which is today!'

'What is Brachytherapy anyway?' I asked.

'Radiotherapy is a sort of gun that emits rays and is aimed at the particular infected area. If the rays don't actually take in all the infected area, or spill over to an unaffected area, tough! However, with Brachytherapy, they pass an instrument up inside the penis and the rays are emitted from the inside.'

My mouth dropped open and he nodded knowingly.

'Hmm, it stands to reason it would be more effective, doesn't it?'

'I would have thought so.' I said.

'Put it like this, if I said to a six-year-old boy: 'Son, you've got cancer in your willy. Now, we can give you Radiotherapy and in five years if it doesn't work, we will cut your willy off, or we can give you Brachytherapy and that will most likely make you better. Which one would you like me to do? Do you think he would know which treatment to choose?'

'Absolutely!'

As the internet was not available to me back then, I had no luck with my inquiries. I tried to get information on Brachytherapy. Even friends who worked in the health service had never heard of it. It amazed me that it appeared to be kept in the dark. Recently, I decided to have a look and found Brachytherapy. I have to say it is not exactly for the faint-hearted but then, if it eradicated cancer, I couldn't care less, it wouldn't have bothered me in the least.

Here's the link to the society in Canada that has posted some videos; (not for the squeamish.) http://www.americanbrachytherapy.org/about-brachytherapy/penile.cfm

To think that they had a system that very likely could have obliterated cancer. Was it because they saved money on the initial outlay? Just thinking about the pros and cons made me seethe.

On Monday morning I phoned David, my solicitor, and explained about Brachytherapy and told him I wanted to sue the Trust again.

He said, 'I shall consult our medical expert on this matter.'

It was a non-starter because our medical expert said: 'We still use Radiotherapy.'

So, it didn't take much figuring out, if he is still using radiotherapy, he's hardly going to say they shouldn't have used it. It made me sick, especially when I recalled Mister Braka saying: 'You had radiotherapy, didn't you? That's old hat, we don't do that here!'

I don't know what became of Ray. When he came, he said that cancer had spread to his lymph nodes. I tried, on quite a few occasions, to ring him but after those initial meetings, I was unable to make contact. I wondered if he had 'run out of time.' There was never any mention of him in the media and I had no idea if his findings were true or not, but even if they weren't, they certainly were food for thought.

How I see all of this is: you are diagnosed with cancer and your treatment is successful. The cancer is gone but not forgotten. You don't feel bitterness about cancer, but relief and gratitude for the wizardry of life-preserving modern treatment. The other side of the coin is; how I and many others suffer so-called medical accidents, which, in my case and numerous others like me, are denied by The Trust. The result is a seething hatred that remains with you forever. It is even more distressing and damaging than the original cancer. When Ray said: 'I'm so angry all the time, I feel like burning the bloody hospital down,' I knew I wasn't alone.

I am so glad that I decided to have the rebuild. I was, without a doubt, one hundred percent right! Had I stuck with Mount Vernon, I would have been so wrong and I am certain I would no longer be here.

Ah well, it's over! It has been done and can't be undone, but I told my sons: 'If ever you have trouble with your penis and are offered Radiotherapy, do try to hold out for Brachytherapy; at least that way you may have a chance.'

At this point, I wondered just how many of you out there have actually heard of Brachytherapy, and how many of you are at present attending hospital with penile cancer and receiving Radiotherapy? And more to the point, how many of you will be back to square one in five years?

A long time afterward, I sat thinking this thing over and concluded that the botched operation actually did me a favour because BXO was not even recognized by Mount Vernon Hospital. They regarded the first op as very successful; and for that matter, so did I! So, if I hadn't had 'The willy chop,' I would never have been referred to Mister Bracka who recognised it, even in the photographs, before he had actually seen it in the flesh, and because of his prediction when he said: 'BXO will see to that!' I know I would either be living in misery minus my penis or, I would possibly have joined the ranks of the unfortunates that my Medical Expert defined so well when he said: 'A large percentage of them commit suicide.'

I also think that if initially I'd had Brachytherapy, which is what I'm sure I should have had, none of this would ever have taken place!

A while ago, this headline was on the front page of the Daily Mail: £10M COST OF GAGGING AN NHS WHISTLE BLOWER. It prompted me to search the net again and I discovered that while my case was in progress, I was completely unaware, as were my (so-called *legal experts*?) 'In December 1994, after my case started and was up and running, a British Airline Pilot was mutilated by a surgeon. He sued the Surgeon for three million pounds. The case went to court and was settled in 1998 ***before*** my case ended!'

The result: <u>10 Most Bizarre Cases of Male Genital Mutilation - ODDEE</u> <u>www.oddee.com/item_98797.aspx</u>. *T*he British Airways Pilot Who was Genitally Mutilated during an Operation (UK) Airways pilot**, was **geni tally mutilated during ...pilot's** penis. **British Airways** James Williams, a former British Airways pilot, who claimed his life was destroyed by surgery to his penis, has settled for damages in excess of £800,000. Further details here: <u>BBC News | UK | 'Mutilated' genitals prompt large pay-out</u> news.bbc.co.uk/2/ hi/uknews/222730.stm In the light of this, should my solicitors hang their heads in shame? Should they have uncovered Mister William's case and fought accordingly for a like sum for me? I certainly think so! He sued the surgeon, not a TRUST where ***everyone*** is gagged by bureaucracy. It was proven that Mister Thomas did the actual cutting!

The headlines (£10M COST OF GAGGING etc.) leave me in no doubt that TRUSTS spare no expense in their defence; millions if necessary. Of course, I think that wasn't necessary in my case, I am of the opinion that my solicitor very successfully engineered a paltry award for me. The unfortunate Pilot did not actually have what the National Dailys described as the 'Willie Chop.' They said that he suffered untold misery, (and I can testify to that; it ***never*** goes away,) but at least he received ***proper*** compensation which is more than can be said for me.

Chapter 5

Our six children have grown up and moved away with families of their own. They are independent and an absolute credit to us. Our adopted children, one of whom was terminally ill from birth, with a life expectancy of two years, died at the age of five. We adopted our other little boy, when he was two, after having fostered him for over a year. He also had severe disability; he is now in his late thirties in the care of the Local Authority as we are no longer able to manage him. We do see him regularly when they bring him on home visits, or we go and take him out for a meal. The other two, one of whom is profoundly deaf, have made their own lives, which is how it should be. We do still see them on occasion. Then we have at least thirty grand and great grandchildren who are delightful and Jeannine, who despite having lived something of a roller coaster ride with me, has stuck with me!

It was also our children who turned what could have been a living hell into a 'Wonderful Life.' They were my rock and are very likely the reason I am still here. I am sure that this article would not be complete if I didn't post a photograph of them also. It is not very often we manage to get them all together, so it is a few years since this was taken, but here they are.

Danny, Nathan, Claire, Seamus, David and Tom

Time marches on and here I am in a photo with Jeannine taken a few years ago.

I do hope that none of you ever have to suffer the same fate that I did. The fact that it had never happened before was quite a problem for me. I was on my own except for my family, there was no one I could turn to for support, guidance, or advice and I'm afraid that the experience of the 'Therapy' that the Lady Surgeon so caringly arranged for me, which later backfired on me during the court case, gave me a very skeptical view of everything termed as: 'in the strictest of confidence.' Consequently, I would never have sought that sort of help either. Anyway, I survived, and all things considered, we have done extremely well and most of it I wouldn't change even if I could.

jimbryansstudio.com